Around Old STRATHAVEN

by
David Pettigrew

The Lanarkshire Yeomanry massed in Common Green, probably just before the outbreak of World War One. The Yeomanry was a part-time volunteer force and each July men from all over Lanarkshire would travel by special trains to wherever their camp was set for that summer.

© 1997 Stenlake Publishing
First Published in the United Kingdom, 1997
By Stenlake Publishing,
Ochiltree Sawmill, The Lade, Ochiltree
Ayrshire KA18 2NX
Tel/Fax 01290 423114

ISBN 1 872074 98 7

The hamlet of Lochar lies south-west of Strathaven, a mile or so off the Muirkirk road. The name of the hamlet is derived from a Gaelic word meaning rushes and it would seem that the land on which it stands was marsh that had to be drained. However, the principal reason for its existence was the Mill which, while no longer in operation, still stands upstream from this view (unchanged today, although the old smithy, pictured here, appears to be undergoing renovation). Producing mostly corn and oatmeal, the mill was powered by a wooden water-wheel until 1890 when the business was strong enough to afford the expense of installing an iron one. The Mill stopped work in 1939 and the building fell into ruin for a time, but is now occupied once more.

The roads into Strathaven from Kilmarnock and Muirkirk converge at Crofthead which has seen considerable development this century. New houses built in the early 1970s have replaced the hedgerows on both the left and right of the picture and the Crofthead cottages, built at some time during the late nineteenth century, themselves have long since been replaced by the Crofthead Garage and Strathaven Caravan Centre. The Garage has been in business for more than forty years and an advert placed in a local guide of the early '60s gives some idea of the services it offered: "Hire drive cars available, MOT testing, petrol, oils, tyres. Have your car serviced by our Most Modern Lubrication Plant. Telephone 3040."

The first landmark on the road to Muirkirk is Brown's Bridge, here being crossed by traction engines employed in the scheme to provide Strathaven with a water supply from Glengavel. The bridge itself was widened and strengthened in 1894 to carry the principal water main from the reservoir to the town and the cottages nearby were built around this time.

Its proper name is Avon Bridge and the original was built in 1703. Before this there was a ford at the site but it is said that after lives were lost in heavy floods, the Duchess of Hamilton ordered a bridge to be built. A toll was set up on the new bridge and Brown was the name of the first toll-keeper.

How long this little village has been known as Gilmourton is unclear, as it is only this century that it has been marked as such on O.S. maps. Prior to 1900 it was always marked as Bowbutts, a reference to the building now known as the Bowbutts Inn. The name refers to the butts used in archery practice by soldiers from Strathaven Castle centuries before. As for Gilmourton, this probably refers to the name of an "erstwhile catechist" who settled in the area at one time.

    Aside from the Bowbutts building and one or two cottages, the village had its own church in the early nineteenth century, although this had disappeared by 1840 and been replaced by a school. This school itself was replaced in 1889 by a new one, along with a school house, and it still takes children from the village and surrounding houses and farms today. The roll has always been fairly small but during World War Two the number rose to over seventy with the addition of evacuees from Glasgow.

A half mile north-west of Gilmourton on the A71 is Ryelands, now the site of a few council houses and Baxter's gift shop and restaurant. Early this century, apart from the station which was opened in 1904, there was a creamery built by the Scottish Wholesale Cooperative Society. Opened in 1907, it processed milk from farms throughout Avondale and its position next to the station allowed much of the milk to be transported to Glasgow - Avondale was famed throughout central Scotland for the richness of its dairy products. It closed in 1939, by which time it was owned by the Milk Marketing Board.

South-east of Gilmourton, and back on the road to Muirkirk, lies Dungavel. Originally the area was an estate belonging to the Duke of Hamilton, and the house, shown here as it was initially designed, was built as his shooting lodge. It was locally known as the Grouse Lodge.

In 1914 the Duke and Duchess vacated their palace at Hamilton (it had to be demolished due to problems with subsidence) and arranged to move to Dungavel. However, alterations and extensions had to be made and the 33 bedroomed mansion soon had a suitably grand turret and battlement to denote its elevated status.

Over the years the purpose of the house has also altered. The needs of the nation at war required that in the First World War the house became a naval hospital and in the Second a convalescent depot for the W.A.A.F. By the 1950s the family were looking to get rid of it and after an attempt to sell it off as an old folks home failed, it became a National Coal Board Training School for young miners. In the 1970s it became a prison.

DRUMCLOG MEMORIAL KIRK & POST OFFICE.

North-west of Dungavel the B745 joins the A71 at Drumclog. This was once merely the collective name for the various farms scattered around a vicinity best-known for the battle fought there in 1679, but in the early years of the twentieth century the community was given more substance by amenities enjoyed by larger towns. In 1912 the Memorial Kirk was built in commemoration of the battle and along with the post & telegraph office, station and school the place became more of a village. Except for the Kirk, none of these facilities exist there now (all closed within the last three decades) and the sort of rural tranquility suggested by the horse and trap is difficult to imagine within the rather savage environment of the A71.

DRUMCLOG STATION ON THE STRATHAVEN AND DARVEL RAILWAY

The Caledonian Railway Company opened their station at Drumclog in 1904. The line closed to both passengers and goods trains in 1939 (by which time it was owned by the London, Midland and Scottish Company), but the station remained open to the mid-1960s for use by occasional localised freight transports. Perhaps the highlight of the station's unremarkable existence was the occasion in 1938 when the Royal Train, containing George VI and Queen Elizabeth, stopped there overnight on its way to the opening of the Empire Exhibition in Glasgow.

The Drumclog correspondent who sent this card refers to this building as "our tin cathedral". It is in fact the predecessor of the 1912 Kirk, and was also known as the 'Memorial' church. Made from corrugated iron, it was erected in 1901 for the area's five hundred or so parishioners who previously had to trek to Strathaven. With the opening of its replacement, the tin church was taken down but found a new use as a clubhouse at the Loudon Hill golf course.

At the Battle of Drumclog, Graham of Claverhouse, the general commanding government troops in the hunting down of religious dissenters, finally took a beating from the Covenanters. Historians have since shown that in many ways the Covenanters were as bigoted as their foes, but the Victorians and Edwardians admired them intensely. Above is the 1839 memorial to the confrontation (actually nothing more than a skirmish, but on the plaque promoted to a full-blown 'battle') and in the background the Seminary of Education which opened that same year, also in commemoration. Services were held on the battlefield on each passing anniversary of the battle, although they were later moved to the Memorial Kirk, and no doubt the kids taught at the seminary were bored to death by endless tales about the bravery and dignity of their Covenanting forefathers. The building was renovated in 1878 and served as a school for Drumclog until 1969 when it had only one teacher and ten pupils; it is now an outdoor activity centre.

That Covenanters were also capable of brutalities is evident from the story of Trumpeter's Well. His men in disarray on the boggy ground at Drumclog, Claverhouse decided to escape back to Glasgow. However, at nearby Coldwakning his horse was brought down by an enemy wielding a pitchfork. With great agility he escaped death by jumping from his dying horse onto the horse of his trumpeter, who was left stranded behind. The trumpeter and others surrendered to the Covenanters and probably thought they would survive, but they were taken to Caldermill and promptly executed, probably at the well (above).

Claverhouse lived to fight another day and continued to cement his reputation as a bogey man of Scottish history. However, many have since thought of him as a hero, including Sir Walter Scott, although he did have certain misgivings. Graham's letters often refer to 'women and shildring' and although he was university-educated therein lies his Achilles' heel. As Scott said, Bluidy Clavers "spelled like a chambermaid".

Until the turn of the century, Caldermill was known as Calderbank. There has been a mill there for at least 200 years so why the name was changed is unclear. It was always tiny but at one time was substantial enough to have its own sub post office and a smithy. The row of cottages appeared around the middle of the nineteenth century and other landmarks of that time included Hillhead farm (which is still being worked today) and the old Calder Bridge.

CALDERMILL, STRATHAVEN.

Calder Mill's principal function was to grind out oatmeal. It was powered by a waterwheel and was in business to 1945 when the last miller was John McStrovock. Very little has changed in Caldermill in the last century and a half and perhaps the biggest event in the hamlet during that time was the arrival of the railway. Because of this the old bridge was replaced in 1904 and the population temporarily rose with the influx of Irish navvies employed on the project.

STRATHAVEN BOWLING GREEN

The area lying to the north of Strathaven town centre contains the town's sporting locations. The Bowling Club was formed in 1862 and today's green is still on the site of the original one. For the first forty years it was only a small green but in 1900, around the time of this photograph, it was extended to full size. A new club house, shown here, was also built at this time, and was given further alterations and extensions in the 1950s and '70s. Money for the club's second green was gifted in 1947 and an additional building has also since been built.

In 1908 land in the Overton district was developed and opened as Strathaven's nine hole golf course. It was extended, with a new club house, to eighteen holes in 1962. It was not, however, the first course in the Strathaven area. That was based to the north-east of town next to Glassford Railway Station and opened in 1897. Mainly used by employees of the Caledonian Railway Company, it closed in 1903.

General View of Chapelton.

Part of the parish of Glassford, Chapelton lies on the A726 to East Kilbride. Always the second village of the parish, it is nevertheless likely to be very ancient as the monks who set up at Glassford in the fifth century are likely to have also established the chapel from which it takes its name. Later this chapel provided an alternative place of worship to the overcrowded church at Glassford and as a result people settled there in greater numbers.

Glasgow Road, Chapelton.

Like everywhere else in Avondale, Chapelton was a fairly isolated farming and weaving community. However, it benefitted from its position on the main Glasgow - East Kilbride - Strathaven road and from 1860 its population began to overtake that of Glassford. As the Rev MacDonald of Glassford said in the 1950s, "Glassford is on the main road to nowhere". Nevertheless, the population of the parish as a whole was falling; from the turn of the century lack of local opportunity meant that most young people left and properties throughout the area were being bought up by retired people and holidaymakers. This may seem like a surprising occurrence for those days but it has always been the way in this part of Lanarkshire. Even as far back as 1720 it was noted that Strathaven itself was populated mostly by old people who moved into town for the convenience of being near the church.

In Chapelton services taken for granted in larger towns such as electricity and sewerage were not provided. Due to low population, and the lack of these facilities, Chapelton almost met its end in 1939. The local authority believed that the cost of installing modern services would be prohibitive and a plan was afoot to have the village shut down, demolished and the community rehoused elsewhere. Luckily, the housing shortage in the immediate post-war years defeated this plan, but electricity and sewerage still did not arrive until the 1950s. Glassford had both at least twenty years earlier.

The old Kirk and Post Office. The office is now based in Main Street, and the Kirk is long gone, although its graveyard is still in use.

Described as thriving in 1792, Chapelton had by then been a village (as opposed to a rural medieval hamlet) for at least a century. The chapel was still in use and the village even had its own minister (rather than one from another church travelling in). However in the eighteenth century the chapel probably fell into disuse and for a time there was no church at all. This changed in 1839 when finally the village's first proper church was built on Main Street. The delay in building this church is likely to have disgruntled the population of around 600 and the lack of attention from the Glassford Kirk Session probably led to their declaring the church a Free Kirk five years later. All the old ecclesiastical ties with Glassford were severed and in 1875 the village became a parish in its own right.

Chapelton Co-op on Main Street (left of centre) was established early this century and later was made the No.2 branch of the Strathaven Co-op. This was the principal amenity of the village, although it also had a Post Office, joiner and blacksmith. The Co-op was in operation until 1983 and became Mrs Callan's shop for the rest of the '80s. It has changed ownership more than a few times since but unfortunately it is now empty. However, there are rumours that it may finally be converted into a house before long.

This chap lounging against a wall in Shawton Road, probably had little else to do but pose for passing postcard photographers. Life in the village was uneventful and even now there are occasional problems with restless youths. Young people have always moved away and in past years a great many went into the armed forces due to the lack of local employment.

New Row (now Road) where the only aspect to have changed is the removal of the thatch from the cottages on the far right.

Because the young people tend to leave, villages like Chapelton have long been a mecca for retired folk and it is largely due to these older incomers that the level of population has been maintained. However, in his entry for the Third Statistical Account of 1951, the Rev. MacDonald of Glassford identified another strand of incomer - the dreaded floating inhabitant who buys local property, stays for a short while doing it up and then sells for a profit and moves on. The Reverend had little time for these people and perhaps he had a point in that they rather dispelled the identity of these once close-knit communities.

Coming back to Strathaven, this is the unchanged view of Overton Road at its junction with Commercial Road. It looks like the coalman is on his rounds, using the transport that was once so common. However, soon after this picture was taken, T.F. Harkness Graham wrote with the utmost surprise: "What is that which in the distance climbs the road like a garish beetle, coloured like a gigantic ladybird? It is the local grocer's bread van - and running, forsooth, without a horse."

Overton lies by the road to Glassford and to the east of the village, on the banks of the Avon Water, Avonholm marks the likely spot of its beginning. On its land are ancient standing stones which possibly date back to the time of the Druids and are the area's oldest relic. In his book, the Rev. Stewart gives an entertaining account of how the druids may have controlled the area before the establishment of the Christian church by intimidating the simple-minded locals with regular sacrifices of local virgins and other deserving types. These vicious ceremonies only ceased when the power of the Druids waned with the arrival of the Romans. Glassford's recorded history starts a few centuries later with the establishment of the Christian church.

The first church at Glassford was built c.430 A.D. by the Monks of St Ninian and the earliest community naturally clustered around the church which was based to the south-east of the present village, roughly at the site of the ruined kirk. The next significant event occurred nine hundred years later in 1296 when the local landowners, the de Glasfords, felt the need for protection and so built a defensive tower at Hall Hill (the gates of Hall Hill House are pictured at the bottom of this picture). The tower was in some way involved in Robert the Bruce's war of independence (Bruce's first pitched battle against the English was fought at Loudon Hill, not too far off, in 1307 and it is likely that men from Glassford fought there) and during the Napoleonic Wars, French prisoners were incarcerated there. It was pulled down in 1828.

A few yards up from Hall Hill, Jackson Street marks the eastern entry into today's Glassford. Locally known as the 'Glessart', Glassford's name has changed three times in its history. Firstly, the old church was known as that of Glasford; then, when buildings began to be erected slightly north-west of the church in the seventeenth century, it was called West Quarter. This name persisted until the mid-nineteenth century when the Post Office was established and it was discovered that there was another West Quarter elsewhere. The village had the choice of taking the parish name and so became Glasford. This particular spelling lasted until the arrival of the railway in the 1860s. The village railway station was built some way out to the west on Station Road (roughly adjacent to the present water filtration works) and apparently the sign-painter misspelled the name with a double 's'. It seems nobody could be bothered to correct this error and ever since the town has been Glassford.

The village appeared in its present position in the eighteenth century as local cottars and weavers began to build their homes away from the marshy land on which the kirk and manse stood. Ministers, such as Hugh Mitchell, who was responsible for the parish's entry in the First Statistical Account, often complained about the damp conditions of their property. However, it appears that Mitchell didn't have anything good to say about anybody or anything and despite the fact that the parish was almost exclusively agricultural he commented, "there is only one man who deserves the name of a farmer". Despite this, the onset of the weaving boom in the latter eighteenth century changed the village's fortunes - in 1771 there were only 65 inhabitants in 14 houses, all cottars with only pigs and hens to their names; twenty years later there were 44 houses and 196 people busy producing cotton, linen and silk, and working at the nearby quarries either as quarrymen or stone masons.

Here the parish church dominates Millar Street, "its spire dark and sombre like a minatory finger against the sky" (more flowery prose from Harkness Graham). The old kirk was rebuilt in 1633 and served until 1820 when this one was opened. Stone from local quarries was used and many of the houses on this street were also put up at the same time. Since then little has changed in Glassford. In Millar Street the most significant changes were the removal of the chimney stack of the building on the right and the building of the Co-op (now a house) on the gap site on the left.

Millar Street looking East, Glassford.

Millar Street again, with the addition of the Co-op. The building of the church symbolised the village's commercial stability. By the mid-1800s the village had a shoemaker, blacksmith, tailor, joiner, baker, butcher, grocer and spirit merchant. The West Quarter Building Society had opened a couple of decade earlier and the Strathaven coach to Stonehouse and Hamilton regularly ran through the village. It can be argued that such self-sufficiency induced a certain insularity in the natives. Although the locals had been involved in the wars of Independence and later with the Covenanter's struggle, the prosperity of the 1800s made them wary of taking risks. It is recorded that the leaders of the Strathaven weaver's rising visited Glassford to drum up support but their cause was treated with indifference by the people there. In the event this was a canny move on their part as the rising was crushed and the leader, sixty year old James Wilson, was famously hanged and beheaded for his trouble.

Alston street contained many of the old weaving shops; indeed one still stands dated 1765. The first houses on both the left and right were demolished in the 1940s as part of the road-widening scheme and it was in this period that the village was extended by the building of council houses prior to and after the Second World War. Although the village has hardly changed, over the centuries the land surrounding it has been denuded of trees. The Parish was once covered in woodland and the name Glassford derives from the old gaelic for "river crossing" and "forest way", i.e. it is a literal description of the hamlet when it stood in a wood by the track that led up from the ford over the Avon.

Like everywhere else, Glassford had a mill. This was situated some distance away from the village at Glassford Bridge, directly by the road between Strathaven and Stonehouse. The miller's cottage still stands as a private house.

The old bridge with the Mill on the right. The mill was established in 1820 and all the local grain was ground there. It was powered directly from the Avon by a waterwheel supported by a dam and a lade. A fairly large operation, it had two sets of grindstones used in the grinding of oatmeal and flour; bran was separated from the flour by sifting it through a bolting machine and there was a kiln for drying the grain. It was one of nine mills in Avondale in 1879 but only two years later it had closed as a flood on the Avon had destroyed the dam. By 1909 there was only one mill left in Avondale, the town mill which eventually closed in 1966.

Glassford Bridge (collapsed Sept. 9th. 1924)

The old stone bridge collapsed, probably through age, in 1924. It was replaced by an iron model which in turn was succeeded by the present concrete bridge in 1970. Bad weather, such as that which closed the mill, may have been a contributing factor, but weather conditions in the area are on the whole distinctly average. The only time the actual village of Glassford has suffered from the weather was in 1938, when a freak storm, lasting only two hours, flooded the village. It was calculated that such a storm could only be expected every 124 years, but for the most part, as the Rev. MacDonald reports in the Third Statistical Account, "rainfall is average; snow a menace; and sunshine moderate".

The furthest outpost of Glassford is the small row of houses on the Stonehouse Road. The area is still rural but such tranquility could not be imagined at the same spot today. Drivers in the area will know full well the frustration of waiting for ages to join the A71 at the bridge junction, the sigh of relief as a pause presents itself, and on turning onto the main road, the almost simultaneous surge of terror as a juggernaut screams over the rise at ninety miles an hour ready to splat anything that lies in its path.

The view from the west of the row of houses at Glassford Bridge.

Bridgeholm, an eighteenth century (or possible earlier) farm and mill, stands on the other side of the A71 from the row on the previous page. The bridge pictured here probably dates from that time but it was demolished and replaced by an iron version early this century.

Todshill Street from the Cross, Strathaven.

Back in Strathaven, Todshill street stands next to the castle just off the Stonehouse road. Although none of the buildings still standing on the street date any earlier than the nineteenth century, the street was originally laid out from the Cross in medieval times and was initially known as Toadshill. Early inhabitants built their houses around the castle for protection and the street was deliberately narrow so that the houses could be defended more easily against attacking enemies. At its widest point the street was only three metres wide. Packed with stores and weaving shops it was usually cramped with inhabitants and traders. This was something of a fire hazard and in 1844 a "great fire" destroyed, amongst other buildings, the street's tannery. Although the Hamilton fire brigade attended, it was only the direction of the wind that day that prevented the fire from spreading to the town centre.

This "grand old character" ambling up Todshill was Jimmie Campbell, a local oldster who toured the town and surrounding area in his cart, selling eggs and poultry. His horse, Maggie, was very popular and apparently had the amazing ability to cock her ears in any direction.

From 1911, Todshill underwent a series of alterations. That year the buildings that flanked the Powmillion Burn were demolished and the street was widened, and in 1935 there was further demolition near the junction with Station Road.

At the Station Road junction, Todshill connects with Lesmahagow Road. Known as Southend until the 1930s, this street, like Todshill, housed many of the town's weavers. Nearby on Newton Road there was also a tannery and a brewery. It managed to escape the earlier fate of Todshill until the 1960s when many houses were demolished, particularly around the junction with Newton Road. The following decade the new Strathaven Fire Station was opened here.

Craig Bridge, Strathaven.

Before the modern A726 was built and the new bridge was erected in 1938, the road to Lesmahagow passed directly over the old Craig Bridge. There has been a mill here since the eighteenth century, although it seems to have gone through intermittent periods of inactivity. The first mill stopped work sometime during the mid-nineteenth century and actually had to be rebuilt in 1869 to become a going concern again. However, this operation only lasted until 1887. Other business concerns at the bridge in the nineteenth century included a separate woollen mill which was intentionally burned down in 1808 and in mid-century a powerloom factory which appears to have disappeared before 1898. Craig Mill itself started work again in 1912 and was run commercially until 1958. The present bridge was opened in 1938.

As a conservation village, very little has changed in Sandford over the past century. There are a number of recent houses but these are situated on the riverbank opposite to Waterside Street and do not interfere with the original layout of the village centre. Aside from these houses, and the post-war building of the school extension, the only other significant change concerns the bridge over the Kype. Old stone bridges such as this were being replaced throughout the early 1900s and similar iron constructions such as its successor are dotted throughout the area covered by this book. The recently completed new bridge is pictured on the next page.

It is likely that Sandford has been occupied since Roman times, but the significant period of growth for the village was probably the latter half of the eighteenth century. The mills on the Kype, Tweedie and Overhall, attracted those who wished to work there and in the main the village was a weaver's community. This community had to have the necessary amenities and tradesmen such as blacksmiths (the Smithy is pictured on the following page) and wheelwrights were also not long in setting up shop.

The first record of houses being built in Sandford comes from 1796 and concerns the building of cottages by James Wilson of Tweedieside Farm. These cottages may have been part of an entrepreneurial scheme or maybe they were simply for his farm workers. The date coincides roughly with the establishment of the mills so some sort of employment would have been available to anyone wanting to settle there.

The view from the eastern end of the hamlet. In the background, the old Roman road which can still be traced to Kirkmuirhill, snakes off in the distance. This was originally a branch route of the main Roman road from Carstairs and possibly reached as far as Irvine. Roman artefacts have been discovered in the immediate vicinity of Sandford and throughout Avondale (graves were found at Craig Quarry in 1860 and on other occasions sandals and coins). The earliest settlers were Romans and as their roads had staging houses built along them (where relay teams of horses were kept) there was probably one at Sandford.

After the Romans came the monks of St Brydes, who established a chapel to the south-west of the village in 1228.

The dramatic scene of change in Sandford! This picture dates from the 1940s when the village had around 100 houses. Next to the school today is the extension, on the site of the now demolished cottage. The swings on the central green have gone and the open ground in front of the cottages on the left is now taken up by their gardens.

Amenities in Sandford were few and perhaps the height of local trade was in 1851 when the village had two blacksmiths, two wheelwrights, three master shoemakers and one shop. The Post Office came later that century and lasted until the 1960s - when speedier services made small offices such as this obsolete. Services were less regulated earlier this century and up to five deliveries of mail were made to local offices throughout the day. Today there are no shops or services left, although a new children's toy centre recently opened at Tweedie Mill.

Old & New School, Sandford, Strathaven.

The first stone bridge was built around the same time as the cottages of 1796 and soon after the village's first school opened in the two-storey house on the right. 77 children, from the village and the surrounding farms, were in attendance here in 1883 and as this number continued to grow a new school (on the left) was built in 1890. The school came under the jurisdiction of Stonehouse Parish who provided the services of the parish minister and district nurse. However, the village has always had stronger links with Strathaven; when buses were introduced in the 1920s the services to Strathaven were much more regular than to Stonehouse and so the locals were much more inclined to make the easier trip into Strathaven for work, shopping or entertainment.

Waterside, Sandford, Strathaven.

Perhaps Sandford's most newsworthy event was a curious tragedy which occurred in 1922. In the 1860s a strange couple arrived to live in the area and built a hut at Whitehill. They were Professor Robert McHardy, a noted Edinburgh composer, and his wife, the Polish Baroness Felice Wielobysca. She had fled Poland in 1860 when the Russians took over and having lost her fortune, she married McHardy who brought her to Sandford where they lived in self-sufficient seclusion for many years. McHardy was the only one who fraternised with the locals and this but rarely. Nevertheless, it was said that they were so devoted to each other that he wouldn't even allow her to tie her own shoelaces. He died in 1921, but the Baroness continued to live in the hut which they had fortified like a castle. She had a ferocious dog and was armed with pistols and daggers to ward off any visitors. Finally the parish council decided that she was a danger and had her arrested. This was a harrowing experience for all involved and the poor woman was dragged off to an asylum while her dog was shot. The mysterious Baroness, who had refused virtually any contact with the natives of her adopted county, died two weeks later.

THE MILL, KYPE WATER, SANDFORD.

Beyond Waterside stands Tweedie Mill (in operation until 1948) and this calm stretch soon becomes a torrent in its approach to the falls at Spectacle E'e. The stepping stones were likely to have been the main river crossing ages before any bridge was built, although they seem to have disappeared today.

As an alternative to the popular theory of how the falls came to be known as Spectacle E'e (detailed on the next page), Harkness Graham suggested that the name may have derived from the Latin *spectaculum*, i.e. 'spectacular' which he evidently felt the falls were. They are indeed impressive, but he rather overstated the issue when he compared them favourably with the Victoria Falls ("one thinks rather of the vulgarity of something big") and goes on to tell how it was at Spectacle E'e that he "leaned down and heard the still music of Eternity".

Sandford's best-known landmark is the Spectacle E'e waterfall. This name comes from the Mill, pictured above in 1894, which once stood beside them. This was probably built in the eighteenth century as a replacement of an earlier mill on the same site which is the subject of an oft-told legend. It is said that a pair of spectacles left on the thatched roof concentrated sunlight on it and subsequently led to its destruction by fire. The pyromaniac involved was a disgruntled youth who positioned the lenses deliberately as vengeance on the miller who would not let him see his daughter, with whom he was in love. By the time the fire had started the lad was well away from the scene and thus had an alibi saving him from suspicion.

Away from the realms of legend, there was definitely a mill on the site as early as 1801, at which time it was known as Overhall Mill. This was a lint and cotton mill (very common in the area) and remained as such until the 1880s when it became a silk and calico printing factory. It was by then famous for its big wheel which Sandford boys believed, erroneously, to be the biggest in Scotland and apparently the noise it made when working was loud enough to drown out the noise of the falls themselves. The mill closed in 1897, probably due to difficulties in transporting goods to and from it, and since then it has lain in ruins.